Hedges and Local History

D1380366

**Published for the
Standing Conference for Local History
by the National Council of Social Service
26 Bedford Square London WC1B 3HU**

© NCSS   London 1971
SBN 7199 0823 X

0719908231X

874, 877

Printed by J W Hemmings and Capey Limited, Leicester

Contents

Introduction

The material in this booklet is published as a result of a one-day conference held jointly by the Standing Conference for Local History and the Botanical Society of the British Isles. The conference was an occasion on which a method used by Dr Hooper to assess the approximate age of an English hedge-bank was introduced to a wider number of local historians and botanists. This method involved a simple count of certain plant species constituting the vegetation of a hedge-bank.

In the contribution made by Professor Hoskins to the conference, he cited sources of documentary evidence against which the validity of Dr Hooper's method might be tested. Professor Bradshaw and Mr Allen suggested means by which Dr Hooper's technique in hedge dating might be augmented through the study of hawthorn species and brambles.

The implications of the possibility of dating hedge-banks from their constituent vegetation should interest local historians. Many English hedge-banks represent ancient boundaries, in some cases going back as far as Anglo-Saxon times. Until now, it has not been possible to determine the age of any hedge for which documentary evidence has been lacking. It is hoped that the publication of this material will encourage local historians and botanists towards joint studies of hedge-banks from which they will gain further knowledge of Dr Hooper's method in anticipation of learning more about the history of their areas.

Hedges and Local History
M D Hooper

Readers of Professor Hoskins' book *Fieldwork in Local History* will know that I believe the most important factor governing the variation in number of kinds of shrub growing in a hedge is the age of that hedge. I have suggested this factor operates in such a way that a hedge which is one hundred years old will usually have only one species of shrub in it, a hedge that is two hundred years old will have two species of shrub and so on, to a hedge that is one thousand years old which will have about ten species of shrub in it.

This suggestion usually arouses one, or all, of three types of reaction or question: the cynical reaction that such a correlation between age and diversity exists only in my imagination; the botanical reaction that such a correlation may exist and the question as to what sort of basic biological process is at work; and the local historian's reaction that such a correlation may exist and the query of what practical use is it? Can one in fact go into a field, count the shrubs and say with any degree of certainty that this hedge was planted in, say, A.D. 950 or even that it was planted at some time in the tenth century?

Does any correlation between age and number of shrubs exist? I originally took 227 hedges which could be dated with some degree of accuracy from documentary evidence and counted the number of shrub species in thirty-yard lengths of these hedges and found a strong positive correlation. The correlation coefficient was $+0.85$ and the regression equation for predicting the age of the hedge from the number of species in a thirty-yard length came to $X = 110 \times Y + 30$. Here X is the age of the hedge in years and Y is the number of species in a thirty-yard length. Strictly speaking this equation gives the age of a ten-species hedge as 1,130 years and not 1,000 years. However, the range of variation is quite large and the limit of accuracy of the prediction is of the order of 200 years. A ten-species hedge can be predicted to be between 900 and 1,300 years old. This is a wide margin of error but it must be remembered that this prediction is based on only just over 200 dated hedges spread throughout the country, from Devon through Gloucester to Cambridge,

Huntingdon and Lincoln. This is a small sample from a large area; it includes many different soils, climatic conditions and local traditions of hedge management. Also the number of hedges included in the calculations which can be dated with any precision in the period between 1050 and 1550 is very small. Hedges dated prior to 1050 were found from the boundary clauses of Saxon charters and for the period after 1550 I used various types of large-scale map, from early estate maps to the modern ordnance survey, with which to date the hedges.

All this suggests that the country-wide correlation is a rather crude one which needs further research. More datable hedges must be found, particularly for the 500-year period between the Norman Conquest and the reign of Elizabeth I.

Nevertheless, there is confirmatory evidence which implies that the correlation will hold even through this period. Different counties have different enclosure histories. It is known for example, that Huntingdon and Lincoln were enclosed much later than Kent, and Kent was in turn enclosed at a later period than Devon. If the correlation is a reasonable approximation to reality the proportions of hedges with different numbers of species in each of these counties should reflect the amount of enclosure in the differing periods. Investigation was made of the proportions of hedges with different numbers of species in them in each of these four counties. The results are shown in the histograms.

In Kent, for example, we found that hedges with only one species in them were rare but hedges with three, four or five species were relatively common. In contrast in Huntingdon and Lincoln most hedges have one, two or three species in them. The most interesting case is Devon: here the data implies that a quarter of the hedges are over 800 years old and that there was a great deal of enclosure some 700 years ago when a further quarter of the hedges were planted. Then, after a lull in the activity there was another spate of hedge planting. I cannot help speculating that the apparent rush to enclose 700 years ago in Devon, or rather the great frequency of hedges with seven species in them, reflects the agricultural expansion in the thirteenth century, that the comparative infrequency of six-species hedges is linked with the decline in population in the fourteenth century and that the rise in frequency in the five-species hedges mirrors a rise in agricultural prosperity in the fifteenth century.

If such broad generalisations on the basis of the botanical evidence are in accord with other historical evidence, then I believe there is a case for accepting the theory that the number of species of shrub in a thirty-yard length of hedge is correlated with the length of time the hedge has existed. The cynic's reaction is justified by some of the detailed evidence but the correlation *is* a reasonable *approximation* to reality.

The botanical question of how the correlation can come about is more difficult to answer. Experimental evidence would be difficult to obtain

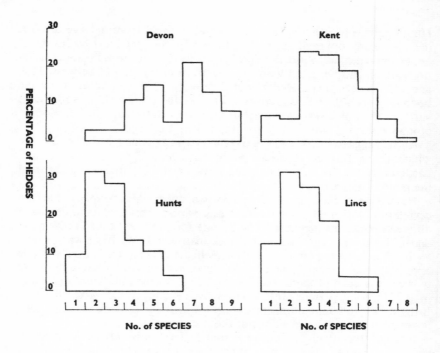

PERCENTAGE of HEDGES

Devon   Kent

Hunts   Lincs

No. of SPECIES   No. of SPECIES

for the experiments would have to run a thousand years. Personally I believe this correlation exists because in a hedge we are dealing with a case of succession. If a piece of bare ground is left alone it reverts from the bare state to grassland and then successively through a tall herb, rough scrub vegetation to the deciduous woodland which, it is believed, is the really natural vegetation over most of the country. Through the intervention of man managing the land this succession can be halted and even deflected from the normal sequence. The most familiar situation of this kind is probably the maintenance of chalk downland through the grazing of sheep and rabbits. If the sheep and rabbits are removed the grassland reverts to scrub and eventually to woodland. A number of such successions have been worked on by botanists and it is commonly found that the number of species increases with age. Usually the relationship between age and number of species is sigmoid; that is the number of species rises slowly at first then more rapidly and finally very slowly again until the natural type of vegetation is reached when the number of species is more or less constant. Linear relationships, such as suggested here for the hedgerows, are not unknown; Doctors van Leeuwen (1936)

8

for example, found a linear relationship in the study of the plant succession on Krakatoa as it settled down after the eruption of 1883.

If the hedgerow is a case of succession then one would expect that some species could occur only at certain stages. Normally an oak tree would not be expected at the grassland stage of a grass-scrub-woodland succession for example. Some evidence of this sort of thing has been found in hedgerows with two species, Field Maple and Spindle. Field maple begins to come in when the hedge already has four species in it; and it is uncommon to find a hedge with field maple and only one or two other species in it whereas it is almost always present in five, six or seven-species hedges. Spindle behaves in much the same way except that it begins to come in when the hedge has six species in it. I infer that a hedge has to be 400 years old before conditions suitable for the establishment of the field maple have developed and similarly the hedge has to be 600 years old before the right conditions for spindle occur.

The chief difficulty over accepting the idea that the hedgerow undergoes succession is the time scale involved. The normal grass-scrub-wood succession is substantially complete in under a century and certainly can achieve a degree of stability in number of species per unit area in a much shorter time. With a hedge however, we are dealing with a linear habitat with little physical space available for colonisation by new species until one of the original complement dies. Moreover, the hedge is, by definition, an artificial habitat subject to management by man.

Management raises yet another difficulty as it is said that some species such as Elder are always removed in hedge management, particularly when the hedge is cut and laid. But elder is in fact more frequent in hedges which have been managed than in those that have not! Indeed in surveys we can find no statistical differences in the numbers of shrubs in various types of managed hedges. Unfortunately we can only speak of recent management. No documentary evidence of the management of a specific hedge in, say, the sixteenth century has come to my notice.

The evidence of the correlation between age and number of species implies that management is not an overriding factor affecting diversity but I assume that it is the continuity of management over the centuries, implied by the modern presence of an old hedge, which causes the lengthening of the time scale of the succession.

The final historical question of what practical application this correlation might have has to some extent been dealt with above. There is a considerable margin of error if one uses the regression equation. This may not be significant if one is interested in separating Saxon hedges from those of a late Victorian Inclosure Award but will certainly prevent any firm conclusions where Tudor and Georgian enclosures are in question. I assume this margin of error is so great simply because the

9

data, used in calculating the correlation and regression equation, comes from such a wide variety of localities. If this is true, then concentration on smaller areas may lead to more precise dating of individual hedgerows. I have tried this in two areas. The first was in Shropshire where I took the ten-kilometres grid square SJ40, covering Church Pulverbatch, Condover and Stapleton, as the test area. This was chosen for me as a test piece by Charles Sinker, the warden of the Preston Montford Field Centre, and it was chosen because the history of enclosure, and the history of agriculture, had been very well worked out by Alec Gayden for the volume of the Victoria County History which has recently been published. A quick reconnaissance was undertaken looking at hedges which were recent enclosures of manorial waste, hedges which were known to have been planted on old open or common field land, and hedges on assart land. I say planted, but they might originally have been cut out of the woodland. We decided that as the period of assarting was between 1100 and 1400 then we should expect six-eight species. The first few hedges we looked at did in fact have this sort of number in them. The open field enclosures were thought to date roughly between 1450 and 1650, and therefore, we thought the hedges should have three to five species. Those first areas we looked at did in fact have these numbers. Late enclosure of the waste, the commons in the SJ40 area, was supposed to date between 1750 and 1850, and this should give us hedges with one or two species, and here the theory started going wrong. Of the early samples that we took — the first few fitted very well. We had two species in hedges which were supposed to have been planted around 1770, but as we went on we found more hedges with four or five species, although we knew these hedges had been planted in, or around, 1800. I was at first quite happy with this. One does get some variation in the period between 1750 and 1850 with landowners beautifying their estates by planting trees; trees which have now gone but which have sprouted from the cut stump giving what appears to be a mixed hedge, when in fact it was originally a single-species hedge with trees. We then took a whole series of random samples within this area. In this series of samples the average number of shrubs, whatever the period of enclosure, was about five. The assarted area samples gave an average of 5.5 species and the common field areas had 4.7, both of which fitted with the theory. But the waste areas had an average of 5.7. This was evidence against the theory working in this area.

I can suggest a reason why it should not work in this part of Shropshire: in the waste areas farmers may have planted three- or four-species hedges to start with. This is what I think has happened, because in this part of Shropshire there is considerable documentary evidence of the planting of mixed hedges. I have been shown seventeenth-century leases which stipulate that mixed hedges should be planted including hawthorn, holly, blackthorn and apple. Then there is Plymley writing the *General View* and in describing the period of enclosure of the commons and wastes he says: 'I enclosed a small common a few years ago, without the expense of buying hawthorns, by taking what grew on the waste already and planting it in a line'. And he specifically mentions three species — hawthorn, holly and blackthorn; so there would have been a three-species hedge to start with in 1800. I spoke with a farmer in this area who said that this is what he would do to plant a hedge even today. In this area, because of this local custom, the dating does break down, even though hedges may continue to accumulate extra species at a rate of one each 100 years.

The second area I have worked on intensively is the triangle of clay upland to the west of Ermine Street, bounded by the Nene on the west and the Roman road between Alconbury and Titchmarsh on the south. In this area there is good documentary evidence of the date of a large number of hedges but again there is a gap in the historical story. There are two Saxon charters with boundary clauses, for Haddon and for Connington, and then nothing precise until the first estate map dated 1541 for Great Gidding. Unfortunately Great Gidding was not enclosed until 1869 and this early map shows very few hedges but from 1600 onward there are a number of maps showing hedgerows on other parishes which can be taken as evidence.

What I have done in this area is to take a dated hedge, count the number of shrub species in several thirty-yard lengths and work out the average number of shrubs for that hedge. Some details for the area are as follows:

1. Great Gidding. Inclosure Award dated 1869. Various maps from 1830-40 show open fields hence only one species in each thirty yards was expected but 1.8 species was the average found.
2. Sawtry All Saints and St Andrews. Inclosure Award dated 1809 hence I expected an average of 1.6 species but found 1.9 species.
3. Coppingford. This has no Inclosure Award, but an estate map dated 1716 shows the area enclosed and other documentary evidence suggests enclosure began in 1652. Hence an average of about 2.9 species was expected and 2.5 species was found.
4. Armston. This parish is believed to have been largely enclosed by 1670 and totally enclosed by 1683. Although there is an Inclosure Act dated 1811 a map of 1716 shows the whole area enclosed with hedges and we can predict an average of 3.2 species. I found 3.5 species.
5. Steeple Gidding. One map of 1648 shows an area of open field and another of 1655 shows it enclosed. The hedges must have been planted about 1650 and I expected 3.2 species and found 3.5 species.
6. Kingsthorpe. This estate is known to have been enclosed about 1570

for sheep ranching and we might expect 4.0 species; 4.1 species were found.

7. Saxon Charter Boundaries. Although these do not specifically mention hedges, I have assumed that the hedges now present on the boundaries must be 900 years old and therefore suggest that 9.0 species should be found. The average turned out to be 8.3 species.

In this area the correlation of one species of shrub to a hundred years seems to be working quite well. By taking several lengths of hedge and working out the average number of shrubs in thirty yards, we get a close approximation to the known age of dated hedges. How can this be put to use?

Monks Wood lies in the extra-parochial district known as Sawtry Judith, formerly the demesne of Sawtry Abbey. Apart from the abbey and a Romano-British site there appears to be no other settlement site except possibly one small area of banks and depressions near the farm known as Whitehall. These hummocks and hollows have been interpreted as a motte and bailey castle, a monastic grange or the original site of Sawtry Judith village. One long hedge runs alongside and I thought shrub counts in the parts most near to the village might give a clue. These have an average of 3.5 species per thirty yards, so what happened in 1620? This we do not know, but in 1608 the Cromwells, who received the estates of the abbey at the dissolution, sold the whole of this area to the Cavendishes. Could it be that a Cavendish, like a new broom sweeping clean, reorganised the field system somewhere about 1620?

Since giving this paper I have received from Dr J. Sheail, via Nottingham University, a photocopy of a map in the Chatsworth archives. This map, dated 1612, is of the estate of the 'Right Hon. William Lord Cavendish, taken by William Senior, Professor of the Mathematiques'. It shows Sawtry Judith and the long hedge referred to above is shown as a boundary between the 'Great Pasture' on the north and several parcels of land to the south which are, from west to east, 'Priest Close', 'Archers Wood', 'Clapper Spring', 'Clapper Yards' and 'Cartir Close'. The area of the suggested village site is 'Clapper Yards' so the hummocks and hollows may be the remains of a warren (*Claperia*=rabbit enclosure) as well as a monastic grange or village site. Whether this warren (and hence the hedge) was established by Sawtry Abbey, the Cromwells or the Cavendishes is still not certain, but the botanical evidence would seem to rule out the abbey.

Another example is right in the middle of the area where nearly all the roads and the streams are parish boundaries. They all seem to run to one point. This point is the Flittermere Pond. I am told 'flittermere' means a disputed boundary, so where is the disputed boundary and when did the dispute take place? The one boundary which takes a sharp curve away from the expected line is the parish boundary of Great Gidding (see map).

12

It looks as though Great Gidding has altered its boundary to gain control of a pond which was once the common property of several parishes. But when did it do it? There are twelve shrubs per thirty yards in this boundary so the dispute took place perhaps, 1,200 years ago and yet is still remembered in the modern name.

In making this study I am indebted to Professor Hoskins who not only drew my attention to a number of early boundaries in Devon but encouraged me to continue with something foreign to my botanical training. Great patience was shown to a crude amateur by a number of county archivists, especially those in the Huntingdon and Northampton Record Offices. Dr Hart, of Stilton, kindly helped with the Saxon charters.

Much of the hedgerow data has been collected by others including my wife in the Devon work and my assistant, Miss Relton, in Huntingdonshire. Dr Pollard collected all the Kent records used here. Many other colleagues at Monks Wood and a number of correspondents have given me records of individual hedges. Without them there would be no theory but if this theory misleads any local historian the fault is mine not that of those who have so kindly helped me.

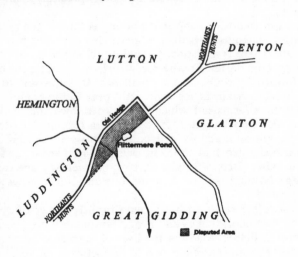

REFERENCES

Doctors van Leeuwen, W. M., Krakatau, 1883 to 1933. *Ann. Jard. Bot. Buitenzorg, 56-57*. 1-506, 1936.
Hoskins, W. G., *Fieldwork in Local History;* Faber, 1968.
Plymley, J. *General View of the Agriculture of Shropshire,* 1803.

Historical Sources for Hedge Dating

W G Hoskins

Even as a young man, and completely untrained as a botanist, it was clear to me that hedges varied greatly in the variety and wealth of their vegetation. I knew a little then about the long series of datable hedges, that they belonged to quite different periods; it was also clear that some hedges were very much more varied than others. I thought that some day it might be possible to date hedges far more precisely than historians alone could do.

I believe I am right in saying that nothing is known for certain about the boundaries of Romano-British estates. This does not mean we shall never find out. There is a distinct possibility of working out these boundaries, and by boundaries I really mean hedges, ignoring all boundaries which are formed by walls, drains or ditches. It is possible to work out the boundaries of certain farms which still bear Celtic names; and I can cite a Devonshire farmstead which is recorded by name in Domesday Book, which also stands right in the corner of a rectangular earthwork of civilian origin, almost certainly an Iron-age farmstead and probably continuously farmed since that time. In one part of Devon (and this may well apply to other parts of England), I would even say one can go back to Bronze-age farming without a break, but this is a long way yet from proof.

The earliest reference that I have found to the practice of demarcating properties by means of ditches and hence presumably hedges, is in a life of the Cornish St Petroc. Many of the lives of the Celtic saints are loaded with myth and legend, but this is one of the better ones, very well edited by Canon Doble. St Petroc died about the middle of the sixth century, in Cornwall, at a farm called Treravel, which is still marked on the map. The biographer says, 'And to guard against the possibility of disagreement with his neighbours arising from disputed boundaries, he surrounded the limits of his lands with very long ditches, dug deep like valleys, the ruins of which remain to this day'. Canon Doble remarks in a footnote that no traces of these trenches seem to remain in the parish of Padstow, which is really Petroc's *stow*. But I feel confident that if a systematic search

14

were made in this area we should probably find some of the boundary ditches drawn or cut in the ground in the early part of the sixth century.

Some of the earliest boundaries for which we can find fairly precise dates are county boundaries. These adopted rivers and streams and ancient roads as far as they could, but there are miles where artificial boundaries had to be made. The question is to find these 'unnatural' bits, and then to establish a date when the boundary was created. Most of my examples come from south-western England for obvious reasons. One can only do this kind of work in a microscopic way, for example the boundary between Devon and Somerset. From the meagre documentary evidence it looks very much as though these two counties were demarcated from each other round about the middle of the ninth century. Similarly with the boundary between Devon and Dorset, and Somerset and Dorset. Wiltshire is first recorded as a shire in A.D. 870 (and of course the word shire clearly tells us what has happened, it has been cut off and marked out). Altogether, to cut this argument short, we can say that many of our county boundaries date from about the middle of the ninth century. There may be examples that do not quite fit, for example Huntingdonshire is first recorded in 1011; but one must not be entirely guided by the accident of the earliest surviving record. I think it is possible to say that most of our county boundaries and the hedges that mark them date from about the mid-ninth century.

Then there is the great body of topographical evidence contained in Anglo-Saxon land charters. Some of the later ones often go into great detail, proceeding from point to point along the boundary of a large estate, again using as far as possible natural features, streams and so on, but more often having to create special boundaries by means of banks and ditches. One case I know of is a deep lane which originated as a double ditch. The ditch was dug out on both sides with a great bank on each side. It finishes up as something that looks like a typical deep west-country lane, especially after a thousand years of weather. This kind of double ditch with a bank each side is frequently an ancient boundary in origin. Dr Hooper inspected one in Devon which was a boundary referred to in a charter of the reign of Athelstan (A.D. 925-39). It carried a date A.D. 670 which presents awkward problems for the historian. A date of this kind used to be dismissed as pure forgery. In fact, to my mind, there is a simple explanation for the discrepancy between date and handwriting. One is dealing with a property which was first marked out in A.D. 670, and re-granted in the early tenth century; in other words a fresh document was made because the original had been destroyed.

One can work out the boundaries of hundreds of such charters which contain details of the boundary points; some will be very interesting because they represent earthworks, ditches and banks created at that recorded date or soon after. One question often put to me is 'How do you know that when the boundary ditch was dug any kind of hedge was planted'. I cannot answer that question except by making two points. First, I think it would be unreasonable, having made a great ditch, not to plant something on top of the bank in order to keep your cattle in, and your neighbours' cattle or wild animals out. Secondly, in Devon at least the vegetation grows at such a pace that it would cover any artificial ditches and banks within a generation. I have seen several modern examples of this fast bush growth in my own lifetime.

There are also, of course, parish boundaries. Almost nothing has been written about parish boundaries; in my opinion, they can be any date between the eighth and twelfth centuries or possibly the seventh, down to the twelfth. I think that period covers the demarcation of most English parishes. They often begin with large mother-churches, embracing a territory with more ancient boundaries, but as the countryside fills up daughter-churches are created with their own territories demarcated inside the old mother-church territory. These parochial boundaries are of a later date; in other words, we have internal division within an original larger area.

Then there is the evidence of minor place-names, which must not be neglected. 'Dalditch' is the name of a farm in East Devon. It is first mentioned in 1210, though I think it almost certainly existed in the time of Domesday (1086). It means 'Dealla's ditch', Dealla being the name presumably of the owner at some early date. On the edge of Dartmoor is a farm called 'Olditch'. The earliest reference is very specific. In 1263 we are told 'Olditch' was the property of Geoffrey *De Veteri fossato* (Geoffrey of the old ditch). If this ditch was already called 'old' in 1263, this is where the botanist must be called in to tell us how old. Place-names should therefore be scrutinised closely, and the earliest references extracted to get a starting point for certain kinds of ditches not otherwise recorded.

Domesday Book (1086) is of varying value for our purposes. It is of immense topographical value in some parts of England, and almost valueless in other parts, depending on the nature of settlement for one thing, and the form of record for another. In the south-west of England and right up the Welsh border, and possibly in Norfolk too, one is dealing largely with a landscape of dispersed settlement. It is possible to use, say, the Devonshire Domesday to put it under a microscope — I have printed the results of this in an essay elsewhere*.

One can sometimes reconstruct the boundaries of the home farm, the lord's farm of 1086, in detail, so that we can look at the hedges of a known boundary of a farm which existed nine hundred years ago. It is

*See Hoskins, 'The Highland Zone in Domesday Book' in *Provincial England* (1963).

16

possible to identify these demesne farms following a number of clues. Then one can, by using the map, identify the boundaries. They are not necessarily the same today as they used to be, but in the south-west it is surprising how often the original boundaries remain unchanged to this day.

The identification of the farmsteads of the villein population — the ordinary farmers as distinct from the demesne farm — is more difficult, but one can still achieve some useful results. From a hedge point of view, therefore, one can say that if this farm existed in 1086 and we know some of its boundaries then we can go to its external or perimeter hedges and say we know this hedge is at least eleventh century in date. How much older than this it is for the botanist to say.

For example, Dr Hooper has produced the results for the southern boundary of the demesne farm of the manor of Cadbury in Devon. This was originally revealed to me by the fact that it was a continuous hedge-line on the map (which is usually a very good clue), a hedge-line that all the other hedges come up to but never cut across. This continuous hedge-line is evidence that it was an original boundary, but I know the farm existed in 1086. Dr Hooper then did his shrub-counting. He counted eleven different species, counting on both sides of the hedge to take account of the different aspects, and said that in his opinion this particular boundary dated from between A.D. 850 and 950, so taking the farm back another century or two before Domesday.

In medieval records, too, one gets a good deal of incidental evidence. Park boundaries are important. They survive in great numbers all over England, above all medieval hunting parks, which are of interest because in hundreds of cases they can be precisely dated. The owner of the land, however important he was, had to get a licence from the crown to make a hunting park, hunting rights being jealously reserved by the crown. These licences are generally recorded in the charter rolls and so give a precise date for the beginning of the park and its boundary banks.

There is, for example, a medieval park in Dorset — Winterborne Houghton. We have not got a precise date of its beginning. A lawsuit in 1294 shows a park existed then and it is still one of the best-preserved medieval deer-parks in Dorset. The bank and ditch are virtually complete to this day. The ditch is on the inside of the bank, to prevent the deer from getting out and wild animals from getting in. The ditch is usually about 7ft wide, the bank is not as impressive as many; but it is 10-15ft wide and 2-5ft high, so from a vegetation point of view it should be of considerable interest and could well give a fairly precise date for the creation of the park.

Then there is the evidence of estate maps which frequently show park boundaries in detail (again by park, I mean the old medieval parks). The charter rolls then give one the licence date for many hunting parks.

Cartularies are a valuable source for the making of boundaries in northern England. On the Pennines one can date some stone walls as a result of disputes between two monasteries and the decision that a wall should be built at a certain place and date to demarcate the disputed lands for ever. There is a good example also in Cambridgeshire where a cartulary records, as a result of a dispute, the making of a ditch with a hedge in 1235. This is called the Beach Ditch, which appears on the map under that name today.

In the register of Leicester Abbey we are told at one point that the abbey had enclosed one of its estates, Ingarsby, which is now one of the best deserted medieval village sites in England. It specifically states that the abbey had enclosed the lordship in 1469 'with hedges and ditches'. So here again we have a precise date to work on, or rather for the botanist to work on.

Most people know that the Tudor period was a time of rapid enclosure. In fact a great deal of the enclosures (in other words the enclosing of the old open arable fields and turning them into pastures) took place in the fifteenth century; most of the damage had been done before 1485. So a great deal of this type of enclosure is rather older than one would think. Nevertheless it continued throughout the Tudor period and from a hedge point of view there are points worth noting. Tudor and Stuart enclosures, down to about 1660, tended to enclose very large fields (some I have seen recorded as 600 acres in size). This meant from a hedge point of view that when farmers discovered by experience (which the modern farmer will discover again in about twenty years' time) that these large areas are very bad for good farming the vast enclosures were cut down to size. A great deal of this was done in the sixteenth and early seventeenth centuries because it was found that large enclosures for sheep and cattle were subject to a number of disadvantages. For instance, one enclosure in Leicestershire of 281 acres was cut down into ten fields, within possibly thirty years of its being made. Once more, then, the perimeter hedges here may be older than the internal hedges.

A vast number of our hedges date from the time of the parliamentary enclosures, roughly the time of George III (1760-1820). Even in Leicestershire, in the heart of the midlands, only 38 per cent of the county remained to be dealt with by George III's reign. The remaining 62 per cent had already been enclosed and hedged. And this is in the Midlands, which we traditionally associate with Parliamentary enclosure, the planned landscape, the planned fields and hedges of the Commissioners. However, it should not be assumed too readily that a date for the enclosure award provides the final answer: that all the hedges in the parish will date from, say, the year after the award. The award nearly always stipulated that hedges must be put up within twelve months; but it cannot be assumed that this is the date for all the hedges of the parish. Some of these awards were really legalising enclosures made at an earlier date. There are plenty of references to enclosures going on in the seventeenth century by private agreement which were not ratified by act of parliament until several generations later. The enclosure award may well be codifying something that had been going on for well over a hundred years.

The second point to make about the enclosure award is that it only stipulated that farmers should put up their perimeter hedges within twelve months. If, for example, a farmer was allotted 120 acres in the award, all he had to do was to put a hedge around the outside of his allotment; but what he did inside this area was entirely his own affair. It might be years before he got around to making the internal hedges.

The great importance of the Tithe Survey should not be overlooked. These maps are some of the finest, and in many cases the earliest, detailed maps we have for most parishes, showing every farm, every field and every hedge. They mostly fall into the 1840s, following the Tithe Commutation Act of 1836. The coverage of different parts of England varies greatly. Cornwall 99 per cent, Devon 97 per cent, Kent 98 per cent (there are reasons for all this) and the lowest coverage is Northamptonshire with only 23.5 per cent. In the south-west and in Kent, and up the Welsh border, the odds are nearly ten to one in favour, but in the Midlands there is only about one chance in three or four of finding a particular map in the county record office.

The immensity of the hedge-mileage in this country, especially in the old-enclosed country, should be borne in mind. In Devon in 1844, John Grant surveyed ten parishes out of 430 as a sample. They varied from very small to very big parishes. The total mileage of hedges was 1,651 and Grant observed that 'in ten parishes the total length of hedges is half as long again as the great wall of China'. In the parish of Crediton alone there were 541 miles of hedge: 'the hedges of this parish would extend from Land's End through the centre of England to Edinburgh in Scotland'. Devon, at this rate, must have had at least 50,000 to 60,000 miles of hedges at that date. We have lost a lot since. Dr Hooper's figures suggest we have lost about a third, but in some parts about 70 per cent has gone in the last decade or so. We are losing valuable evidence at a great pace, apart from all other considerations.

The Significance of Hawthorns

A D Bradshaw

To understand the history of our hedgerows Dr Hooper has produced evidence which is dependent on examining the numbers of species which have come into hedgerows on their own by the natural processes of seed dispersal. With such powerful evidence it does not seem likely that we could get any useful information out of the species that were planted to form the hedgerow in the first place, since these would have been picked arbitrarily by the men who planted them. But on reflection this cannot be true, for the material that was used was obviously that which was most ready to hand. So there is every reason that the constitution of hedgerows should reflect the local materials that were available at the time of planting, as our houses and cottages reflect their local materials. When with the passage of time the materials for making hedgerows changed so should have the hedgerows, just as Cotswold stone and brick are being replaced by standardised bricks and concrete.

The major species that make up our hedgerow, and was planted, is the hawthorn or quick. There are two species. The commonest is *Crataegus monogyna Jacq.* It is very widely distributed throughout Britain. It has divided leaves, one stile and one stone in its fruit, many small flowers, and it tends to be more spiney. The other species is less common. It used to be called *Crataegus oxyacanthoides Thuill*, but is now more properly called *Crataegus laevigata (Poiret) D.C.* Its common name is the midland thorn, and it is in fact found rather more in the Midlands particularly on the heavy clays, such as the Oxford and Kimmeridge Clays, and the Keuper Marl, which are so abundant. It can be distinguished by its leaf shape, which is almost entire like a plum, and by the two or more stiles and two stones to its fruits. There are a number of other subtle characteristics; it has fewer, bigger flowers, and many serrations to the edges of the leaves.

The two species not only have distinctive geographical distributions, they also have distinctive local ecological preferences. *C. monogyna* is typically found outside woodlands, in open spaces particularly, where it behaves as a scrub plant. *C. laevigata* on the other hand is found mostly

20

in woodlands on heavy clay soil. The differences between them are particularly visible in woodlands. In a woodland, *C. monogyna* behaves like a tree; it grows straight up, with few side branches, and keeps most of its canopy up in the light. Its leaves are arranged irregularly at all angles: it has not got a good leaf mosaic. It does not seem adapted to shade conditions at all. *C. laevigata* on the other hand behaves very differently in a wood. It grows quite well under trees and maintains many low leafy branches well below the normal tree canopy. It has a very good leaf mosaic.

The flowering of these two species in a woodland confirms the differences between them. In Buff Wood in Cambridgeshire where the two species were growing side by side there were forty-four plants of *C. laevigata*, of which twenty-two flowered; sixteen of these were in margins of the wood. There were forty-seven plants of *C. monogyna*, of which two flowered; both were in marginal habitats.

The species are obviously very distinctive and are 'good' species. They have a constellation of characters which differentiate each from the other. They must have had a long evolutionary history apart. But the situation in nature is not quite so straightforward as this. Although there are plenty of populations which are composed of one or other species by itself, there are other populations where the species occur together. In these populations many plants can be found which combine the characters of the two species. Many of these are strictly intermediate, but some are intermediate for some characters and not for others. There are other populations which seem a complete mixture, with many intermediates (Fig. 1).

If it is possible to find pure populations, and also mixed ones, the most obvious explanation is that there are two originally distinct entities which have somehow got muddled. This in practice means that somehow the entities can hybridise with each other and form a mixed population in which there are not only first generation hybrids, but subsequent generations in which the original parental characteristics have been recombined (Bradshaw, 1953). If this is true, the first essential is to demonstrate that they will hybridise, and secondly that the hybrids that have formed are capable of producing further generations. If this is so then the mixing process can go on. In experiments where *C. laevigata* was pollinated with pollen from other plants of the same species, the seed set was about 50 per cent. The same applied when *C. monogyna* was pollinated with *C. monogyna*. When *C. laevigata* was crossed with *C. monogyna* or the reverse the seed set was again the same (Table 1). So there seems no isolation between the two species.

To find out whether the intermediate types (which we now presume are produced by hybridisation) can produce further generations we must know if they are fertile. The easiest way to do this is to look at the pollen

21

Table 1. Seed set in crosses between *Crataegus monogyna* and *C. laevigata*.

No. of crosses and selfs					Flowers Pollinated	% Fruit set
10 C. laevigata x C. laevigata ...			...		174	59
11 C. monogyna x C. monogyna			...		135	53
12 C. laevigata x C. monogyna			...		194	30
11 C. monogyna x C. laevigata			...		170	45
12 Selfs ...	...	...	...	...	199	2

Similarly for crosses including intermediate types.

of a whole range of types with different amounts of leaf indentation. In plants sterile hybrids can be spotted by the pollen which is misshapen and empty. Fig. 2 shows that although there are some intermediate individuals which are partially sterile there are a vast number of intermediate individuals which are perfectly fertile. There is no sign of hybrid sterility, and this is borne out when the fruit is set: intermediate plants produce fruit as readily as the pure species. So there is no evidence for any real barrier between these two species, and I think one can presume quite reasonably that they hybridise readily, and form what is known as hybrid swarm. The only barrier between them is that one normally lives in a woodland, and the other one lives in open spaces. Providing the environment is not disturbed these two will be kept quite separate from one another but in disturbed areas the isolation between the species can readily be broken.

This can be tested by comparing populations in sites with different degrees of disturbance. The simplest way to do this is to examine hawthorn populations for one character only, that of the amount of leaf indentation. This is best expressed as a ratio of the total lengths of indentation on one side of the leaf to the length plus breadth of the leaf. By this method populations of pure *C. monogyna* coming for instance from chalk down have mean values of about twenty-eight and populations of pure *C. laevigata* coming from dense woodland have mean values of about ten. The difference between populations of the two species is considerable (Fig. 3). The purity and distinctiveness of these populations can be explained by the fact that in these two cases, the other species is some distance away, so there is spatial isolation.

However it is possible to find hawthorn populations where the two species have been allowed to come in contact by disturbance, for example on the edge of woods. The difference between the hawthorn population in the middle and at the edge of Buff Wood is very marked (Fig. 4).

In woods which have been subject to disturbance throughout, mixed populations can extend right through the wood. Hardwick Wood, near Cambridge, is a good example, it has an enormous range of variation. Similarly, in the scrub areas that have grown up just outside some of these woods, there is the same shambles. Croydon Wilds is an area of scrub which grew up on heavy clay in the agricultural depression in the 1930s, and is not far from woods containing *C. laevigata* (it is about one mile from Buff Wood and Haley Woods). In this scrub there is a large preponderance of *C. monogyna*, but there are a great deal of intermediates and *C. laevigata* (Fig. 4).

Since *C. laevigata* is the hawthorn of woodland and *C. monogyna* the hawthorn of open spaces, and with the passage of time the woodlands

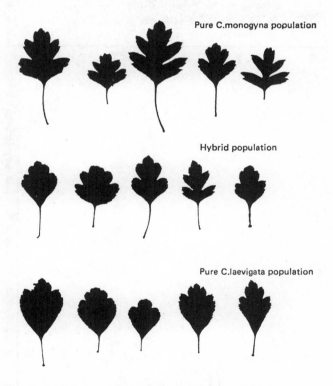

Pure C.monogyna population

Hybrid population

Pure C.laevigata population

Fig. 1. Leaves of pure and mixed populations of *Crataegus*. Each leaf is representative of a single plant.

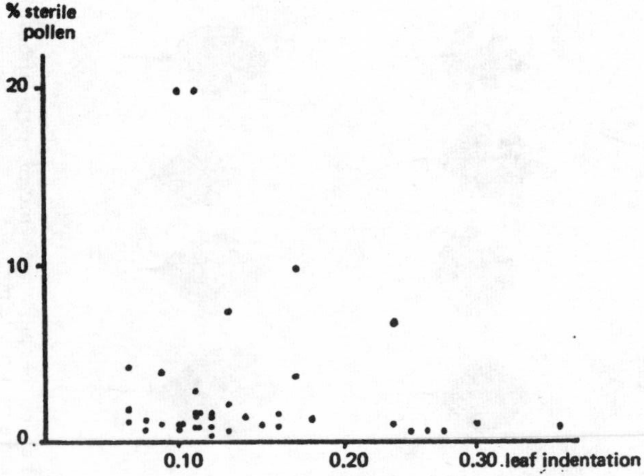

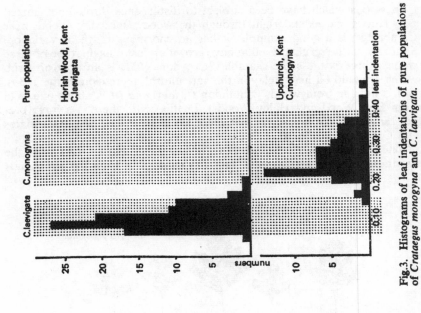

Fig.3. Histograms of leaf indentations of pure populations of *Crataegus monogyna* and *C. laevigata*.

Fig. 2. Pollen fertility of individual plants of the two species of *Crataegus* and intermediates between them (type of plant indicated by amount of indentation: see p. 23).

24

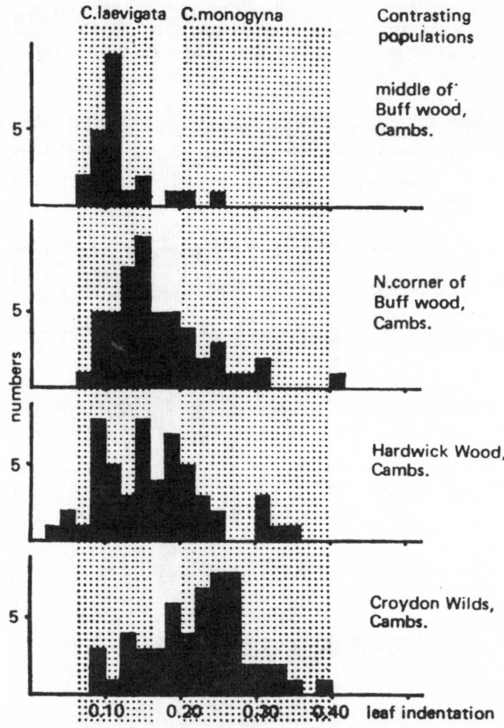

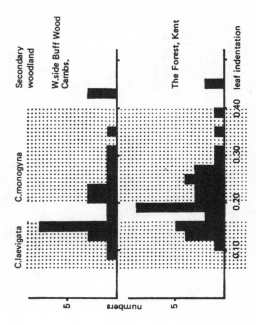

Fig. 5. Histograms of leaf indentation of populations of *Crataegus* in secondary woodland.

Fig. 4. Histograms of leaf indentation of populations of *Crataegus* differing in degree of disturbance (range of pure populations of *C. monogyna* and *C. laevigata* indicated).

25

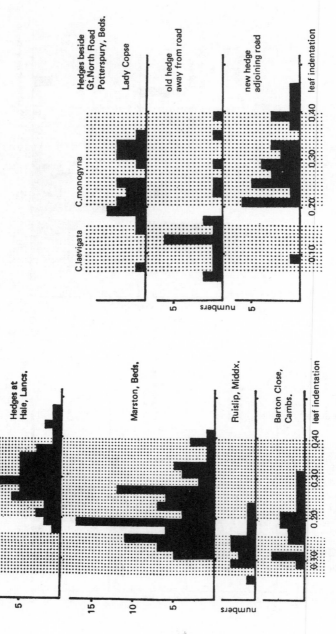

Fig. 6. Histograms of leaf indentation of populations of *Crataegus* in hedgerows outside and within the geographical distribution of *C. laevigata*.

Fig. 7. Histogram of leaf indentation of populations of *Crataegus* in hedgerows of different ages. (a) beside Great North Road, Potterspury, Beds.

26

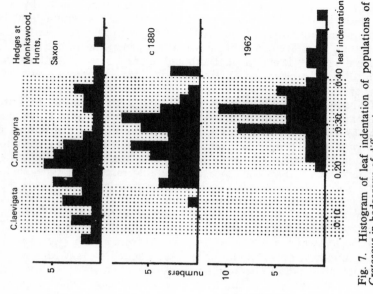

Fig. 7. Histogram of leaf indentation of populations of *Crataegus* in hedgerows of different ages. (b) beside Saxon Road, Monkswood, Hunts.

are being reduced and more disturbed, the hawthorn populations of the country must be changing in the direction of *C. monogyna*. This will be occurring not only by the incursion of pure *C. monogyna* into the populations, but by its hybridisation with *C. laevigata;* the latter is called introgressive hybridisation. It is unlikely that populations are changing anywhere in the reverse direction.

The life of *Crataegus* is very long. If it is cut back as in coppice or in a hedgerow, it sends up new shoots from the base, which have their own root system. It is impossible to specify but there seems no reason why under these conditions a hawthorn cannot last indefinitely, for very many centuries. So the pattern of hawthorn populations is not just a reflection of present conditions, but can be an historical record of the past. In any situation whether it is woodland or hedgerow there will be recruitment going on up to the present day. But the composition of the hawthorn population seems likely to reflect very closely the conditions and the species available when it first arose. Buff Wood west side and the Forest are both secondary woodland developed on old arable land. They have very mixed populations which are likely to be the populations which appeared when the wood grew up (Fig. 5). It is very likely that more historical correlations of this sort would be found for woodland populations.

One very obvious place where hawthorns grow is in hedgerows. Because of their spines and the ease with which they can be reproduced by cuttings or seeds they are ideal material for keeping stock within bounds. In Britain hawthorns have been used for hedges to the exclusion of almost everything else. We can then ask what sort of hawthorns are to be found in these hedges? It is clear that although there is slow continuous recruitment of new species from Dr Hooper's evidence, hedgerows must mainly consist of the hawthorns with which they were originally planted.

In hedgerows where there is no *C. laevigata* such as in the north of England, outside Liverpool, hedgerows are always pure *C. monogyna* (Fig. 6). But in the South Midlands within the area of distribution of *C. laevigata* some hedges are very different, such as on the road to the Marston Brickworks and two other roadside hedges in Ruislip and Cambridge. These hedges contain a considerable mixture of types including some plants which are indistinguishable from *C. laevigata*. Where did this *C. laevigata* come from? It is now a long way from any source of material, for in the area *C. laevigata* is now restricted to woodlands several miles away, yet there is plenty of *C. monogyna* about. Either the material of *C. laevigata* which was planted was carried from a long way away, which seems unlikely, or when the hedge was planted *C. laevigata* was more common and ready to hand in neighbouring woodlands. Such woodlands would only have been common several centuries ago, which suggests the hedges are very old. But we have no date for them.

We can progress further. One or two astute botanists have in the past noticed that the hedges do differ in their *C. laevigata* content. For instance *The Flora of Leicestershire* for 1886 says that '*C. laevigata* is most frequent in old hedges, especially on the eastern side of the country — all the more recent planted hedges appear to consist of *C. monogyna*'. This is well illustrated by the hedges along the side of the Great North Road at Potterspury. Here the road runs through a wood, Lady Copse, on its west side. There is a hedge forming the boundary to the wood close to the road which is pure *C. monogyna*. But about fifteen metres from this, now in the wood itself, is another hedge running parallel to the road for a long distance, which is much more mixed and with characteristics similar to the hawthorn population in the wood itself (Fig. 7a). There are many good reasons why in past centuries roads had to be kept wide, such as protection from highwaymen and the need for the coach to be able to choose different tracks in wet weather. The fact remains however that roads in heavy clay and wooded regions were originally much wider than they are now, and have only become narrow recently. The land released has gone back into agriculture, often in the form of long thin fields parallel to the road. These fields like all others are bounded by hedges, which, because of their origin, will be of different ages. In the case of the hedges beside the Great North Road it is significant that the historically older hedge is the one with some *C. laevigata* in it. At the same time the woodland population betrays that it is not very old. It is a very hybrid mixture. In fact the wood has ridge and furrow through it and must be secondary, grown up over arable land. There is a suggestion from the hawthorn population that it is younger than the old hedge. This is very reasonable, since the road itself is of Roman origin.

It is quite clear that there has been in historic times the change from the one type of hedgerow population to the other, and one would like to know when. Presumably it happened when the source of hawthorns became restricted, when transport became easier, and men became more selective. They changed from picking up bad local hawthorn to picking up good *C. monogyna* material.

Dr Hooper is now providing dates of planting for a large number of hawthorn hedges which are conveniently within the area of *C. laevigata*. An analysis of three of them — one lying alongside a road known to be of Saxon age, outside Monkswood Experimental Station, another running away from it at right angles known to have been planted at the time of the enclosures, and the third planted only a few years ago — shows that the change to typical *C. monogyna* material had taken place by the time of the enclosures (Fig. 7b). The younger hedge was possibly planted by hawthorns raised by Laxton, who, although famous for his apples, made his money in providing material for Enclosure Act hedges. The youngest hedge shows that modern nurserymen have selected parental material of *C. monogyna* which is even more dissected, possibly because it is more spiney, or at least looks as though it is. Recent hedges made of such extreme material are now quite common.

It is unlikely that there will be one fixed date when the change of planting material from *C. laevigata* to *C. monogyna* occurred, but it should be possible to get some idea and perhaps relate it to historical and ecological factors. At least at the moment an examination of hawthorns allows us to distinguish between hedges of different histories, and to say which is older and which is younger. We hope it will soon provide us with much more, and become yet another, if rather curious, key to the past.

REFERENCES

Bradshaw, A. D. Human Influence on hybridisation in *Crataegus*. In *The Changing Flora of Britain* (ed. J. E. Lousley), Botanical Soc. Brit. Isles, T. Buncle, Arbroath, 181-183, 1953.

Mott, F. T., Carpenter, E. F., Cooper, E. F., Finch, J. E. M., Cooper, C. W. *The Flora of Leicestershire*. Williams and Norgate, London, 1886.

Bramble-dating: A Promising Approach

D E Allen

Once again I see
These hedge-rows, hardly hedge-rows, little lines
Of sportive wood run wild.

These famous lines from Wordsworth's *Tintern Abbey* remind me of a fact that is often overlooked; the true hedgerow, populated with shrubs and scattered trees and as often as not with a rich array of herbs in the hedge bottom and on the bank below, is essentially an English phenomenon. To the north and west, in the so-called Highland zone, where the soils become for the most part slatey and acid, what passes for a hedge-bank bears but a slight rèsemblance to what an Englishman understands by that term. Typically, the 'hedge' in the north and west is a sod bank, commonly quite high and extremely sturdy, surmounted with a prickly shrub, which is very often the common gorse. Only where the soils are less acid and in sheltered areas of relatively recent settlement do we find hedges on the English pattern — hedges in the sense of full-scale palisades of greenery, as opposed to protective dykes with an upper, thorny portion. Gorse grows well on these thin, acid soils. And so do brambles. Apart from wild briars, brambles are in fact virtually the sole spontaneous shrubby species of any frequency (for the gorse has been mainly, if not entirely, planted).

This is the other way in which these northern and western hedges are distinct. They not only have a basically different structure; their wild flora is far more uniform. There are fewer flowering plants in the British flora, in any case, that like acid soils (as opposed to neutral or calcareous ones); on top of this, the number of species, as one might expect, thins out considerably towards the further periphery of these islands, as one enters a more generally inhospitable climate and as one goes away from their original point of entry into this country from the continent subsequent to the Ice Age.

This poverty of species means that the technique which Dr Hooper has described inevitably breaks down outside Lowland England. Throughout the north and west there are simply not enough kinds of shrub according to his criteria — and note this qualification — to permit the rule to operate. And the non-shrub species are no better: monotonous stretches of bracken, bluebells, foxgloves, a few standard grasses — very little else. The northern and western hedgebanks are often brighter and gayer, they *seem* richer; but in reality they lack the important diversity of their Lowland English counterparts.

For some years now I have been studying intensively the flora of the Isle of Man. The hedgebanks there are overwhelmingly of this non-English type, for most of the island consists of slate and the farming practices, from time immemorial, have been much the same as those in Ireland, Scotland and Wales. For the botanist in search of the more uncommon species the hedgebanks are dull, and one quickly turns one's back on them in favour of more promising habitats. Indeed, I suspect that I should never have looked at them again with anything more than the most cursory interest, had I not happened to become caught up in that alluring intellectual thicket that has caught many another local flora writer before me: the brambles.

The brambles, or blackberries, are one of the great problem-groups of the British flora. For at least a century and a half people have been aware that there are numerous different kinds, that the species which Linnaeus originally (and very optimistically) christened *Rubus fouticosus* is in reality a huge conglomeration of hundreds, if not thousands, of true-breeding lines, each with its own distinct local or regional distribution. At first, people simply refused to believe that nature could be as perverse and complicated as this. Nothing was known of the mechanisms that cause such variation, and it was generally assumed that a species was a clear-cut entity whose distinctiveness was transparently obvious to even the most casual observer. To the great majority, in any case, the differences apeared so minute as scarcely to be worth bothering with — even supposing that they could see them at all in the first place.

Perhaps the Isle of Man was an ideal area to start: there were just enough different kinds to whet one's appetite and stretch one's mind, yet not so many, for the most part, in any one place to baffle and demoralise one in the crucial early stages. Most people, I suspect, are unfortunate enough to start in a part of the country where the forms are much more numerous and so more swamping for the unpractised beginner.

The early investigators of the group tried to persuade themselves that the variation they encountered could be fitted, albeit untidily, into just a few very broadly-delimited species. As work progressed, however, this was seen to be untenable. The broad species were manifestly artificial clumpings. Clearly, if names were to be applied, far more than previously would have to be allowed. As the country came to be more thoroughly explored, more and more new entities were discovered and had to be described. As a result, when the late W. C. R. Watson's monograph of the group was published in 1958 no less than 387 species were accepted as reliably recorded for the British Isles alone — and Watson, we are assured by the experts who have come after him, was himself much more

31

of a 'lumper' than most people have realised, insisting on identifying British forms with somewhat similar forms on the continent to an extent that is now regarded as indefensible. Probably, therefore, there are well over 400, and maybe over 500, distinct entities of this kind in these islands. Most of them, though, are more or less highly localised: some confined to a single wood or heath; many found only in the West Midlands, say, or Yorkshire or Ireland; a very high proportion known only from the far south of England. In the more outlying areas, accordingly, the number of species is by no means unmanageable. After several years exhaustively combing the Isle of Man I have succeeded in finding no more than forty-five. In the much larger, and geologically more diverse, county of Staffordshire and over a much longer period Mr. E. S. Edees, currently our foremost national authority on the group, has come up with rather more than twice that total.

It may be argued that these entities are not 'species' in the normal sense and that to use this term for them is merely to debase our classificatory coinage. But if these entities are accepted as worth studying, then they must receive a name, or alternatively a serial number; and a name, after all, is the easier to remember and to use in communications with others. And if it is accepted that a name is necessary, then I cannot see that the standard twosome, genus and species, is so objectionable that we should forego its unique convenience. All that matters is that, in borrowing this terminology, we should be quite clear that we are talking about entities of a very special kind.

They are special because almost all of them reproduce partly or wholly asexually. Asexual reproduction means that a plant can produce good seed without requiring to be fertilised; as a result numerous minor strains, which in ordinary circumstances would quickly lose their distinctiveness under the impact of inter-breeding, are enabled to survive in perpetuity. These strains thus enjoy the autonomy of ordinary species: they are, as it were, 'mini-species'. But unlike some of the other problem-groups in our flora, which reproduce *entirely* asexually, brambles do, on occasions, produce offspring capable of forming fertile hybrids. In this way new entities, from time to time, are created, which proceed to colonise a district. This process, however, being fraught with a good deal of hazard, is not, apparently, very common and for the most part we seem to be dealing with entities that have been in existence since time immemorial.

What is more, brambles are shrubs — and, as such, long-enduring in the places in which they occur. They are not at all easily eradicated; no one ordinarily wants to remove them for commercial or ornamental purposes; their prickliness saves them from a lot of casual trampling and bruising. Still better, they spread vegetatively in a most robust and vigorous fashion, by means of offsets formed at the tips of the main stem

32

and its branches. This tip-rooting seems, in fact, to be the principal form of propagation and accounts for the strikingly continuous distribution of so many individual bramble species — all along one hedgebank for hundreds of yards, for example, or (like one species in the Isle of Man) solidly occupying the best part of half a square mile of country but found nowhere at all outside it. Seedlings *are* produced as well, often in quantity, especially where birds perch with any regularity; but they cannot stand much sunshine and are subject to all the many vicissitudes that are the fate of seedlings generally. Common observation suggests that this is not the primary mode of spread. Bird dispersal is essential for the colonising of quite new areas: tip-rooting comes into its own for the building-up of colonies, once the initial immigration has taken place. Beside these, a third mode of dispersal exists — though by comparison with the other two its extent seems negligible. This is accidental introduction into gardens with transported soil, with perhaps subsequent invasion of the adjacent wilds. Insofar as this allows some species to leap natural barriers — in colonising islands for example — or permits others to colonise quite new areas far earlier than would have been possible with the normal rate of natural spread, its importance is doubtless out of all proportion to its frequency.

Armed with all these advantages, why have brambles not covered most of the countryside to a depth of several feet? One major answer seems to be — rabbits. At the time of the outbreak of the recent myxomatosis epidemic, people were astonished to observe the extraordinary luxuriance of the brambles in the season immediately following. Rabbits, it seems, feed on the tender stem shoots and the seedlings, keeping these plants effectively in check. But as there were none of these creatures in Britain previous to Norman times, what, one wonders, kept the brambles down in days before then? It may well be that in earlier periods the dispersal rate in brambles, in the absence of any equivalent adverse pressure, was in consequence more rapid — and this is clearly an important point to bear in mind in any attempt to employ these plants as a dating device.

When I began the study of brambles, my overriding concern was geographical. My aim was to find as many different kinds as possible in the island I was exploring, in the hope that a recently-evolved (and perhaps still evolving) group such as this would provide a more sharply suggestive pattern of affinity with one or other of the four countries bordering on the Irish Sea than I had so far been successful in detecting among the more ordinary flowering plant species.

After two years' work I began to notice a curious thing — without, to begin with, thinking about it very hard. Certain minor lanes, not obviously different from their neighbours, proved to be unexpectedly rich in species, possessing instead of the normal three or four as many as eight or nine, over impressively short stretches. In addition to the standard three or four species that are common to very common over most of the island, they had, besides, a surprisingly complete share of the three or four others that were at all widely distributed in the particular district concerned. In one or two cases, as well, they harboured a species not or hardly at all found anywhere else in the island. They were, so to speak, cases — but of a peculiarly unpredicted kind.

My first thought was that these were 'hinge areas', unusually well-blessed in their flora thanks to the accident of their being situated where two climatic districts, sufficiently different from one another each to have its own small quota of distinctive species, met and narrowly over-lapped. To a limited extent this explanation may indeed be true. After a time, however, I spotted a characteristic of these lanes that at first I had quite overlooked. Several of them, despite a generally unkempt and neglected appearance, were abnormally wide and stately, as if they had once led to somewhere rather important — although now, as often as not, they led nowhere at all in particular. Their banks, too, tended to be high and heavily overgrown. And the lanes themselves were invariably un-metalled. They were, it seemed, 'ghost roads' — with a vegetation of living fossils.

I should perhaps add that hedges of old lanes are not the only places in Man where bramble species occur in exceptional concentrations. They also occur like this in the grounds of the old demesnes, where landed gentry were established for many generations and imported innumerable plants to improve their appearance. These areas have accordingly acted on the one hand as reception centres for accidental introductions and on the other as refuges for indigenous species with a liking for shade and a soil that is not too inhospitably acid. Apart from these, there is one other habitat with an astonishing array of bramble species: a small sheltered ravine and the gently-sloping cliff-face to one side of it half-way up the east coast of Man. Here thirteen species occur, two of them nowhere else. I am quite at a loss to explain this. The area seems hardly abnormal enough in any way to account for such an extraordinary assemblage. Just conceivably, it was cleared by man very early on and bramble-eating birds have been attracted here in peculiar abundance. But this is the wildest guess.

The next part of the story took place in Ireland. In 1961 I was touring the southern half of that country with the idea of seeing for myself how far in fact the Irish flora resembled that of Man. One typically Irish 'soft' day found me marooned in a somewhat indifferent hostelry a few miles outside Limerick; and, to comfort myself, I began glancing through a copy of *Irish Heritage*, by Professor E. Estyn Evans. And in this I stumbled across the vital clue. Writing of the various types of fences that one encounters in the Irish countryside, the author remarks that the oldest ones of all are represented by protective banks round farms occupying old village sites and also by the march-dykes, or divisions between town-lands. He goes on to say: 'The varied vegetation of these older banks betrays them just as it does the pre-enclosure hedgerows in England: their massive tumbled ruins are overgrown with whins, blackthorn . . . and bramble'. With bramble — that was the trigger. 'Massive tumbled ruins': the hedgebanks in my mysterious Manx lanes, of course.

But what made me even more excited was a tantalising reference to some old field fences up in the hills in Co. Limerick which a leading Irish archaeologist, Professor O'Riordain, in the course of excavations in the mid-1930s, had apparently conclusively demonstrated belonged to the period of the raths — that is to say, to the late Bronze Age. These old fences, it appeared, are closely followed by the field-boundaries of today, suggesting that some at least of the Irish sod fences have a strikingly long history of continuity.

This was a revelation. It had never occurred to me before that hedges could date from as far back as prehistoric times. How wonderfully elegant, I thought, if we can use their bramble composition to help us to sort out the old from the recent and to provide us with quick indicators of those that merit more careful investigation. Thus was born the new science of bramble-dating — or, as I prefer to term it, with proper scientific gravity, 'butochronology' (by analogy with 'butologist', the word long since coined — from the Greek *Batos*, a bramble — and traditionally used to designate a specialist in this genus). Although I claim to have invented it myself, I would like to take this opportunity of acknowledging my original debt to Professor Estyn Evans and his remarkably erudite and penetrating book.

When I returned to Man the next year, I saw a great deal that had pre-viously escaped my attention. It was at once apparent, for example, that the older stretches of the main roads had a bramble flora perceptibly more diverse than the modern bypasses; while the main roads, in turn, were altogether less rich in species than the secondary ones which in so many cases are the main roads of yesterday. Richest of all were the lanes which — as far as we can tell — apparently follow the route of ancient trackways. On one of these, in particular, I had been much struck by the singular concentration of less common species, together with one found nowhere else and still to this day unidentified. I now realise that this lane formed part of the old road from Kirkmichael, one of the main northern villages, to Tynwald, the sacred mound in the very centre of the island on which the Manx have by long tradition held their open-air national assembly — in other words, it was part of one of the trunk routes of prehistoric times. This road is believed to go back at least to the Iron Age and may be far earlier; and it is not therefore very surprising that, with hedgebanks perhaps as old as this, a more than ordinary stock of bramble species has had the necessary time to accumulate.

Not being resident in the island and having had to cram my entire annual fieldwork there into usually no more than two weeks, I have postponed the laborious process of sifting and testing my preliminary observations by means of documentary evidence. My work has thus not been pressed through to its logical conclusion in the same way as Dr Hooper's. Before long I hope to return to the Manx hedges in earnest; and, if my hunch is right, it should prove possible to turn up some hitherto overlooked data of value to the local historians and archaeologists.

What I am offering, in effect, is an auxiliary scheme to that proposed by Dr Hooper. For it will be obvious that, *if we count in all the different kinds of bramble as well,* the number of shrub species on which we can draw for hedge-dating purposes is at once expanded enormously. In short, in those areas — such as the north and west of the British Isles — where the variety of other kinds of shrub is too restricted to make the normal dating technique feasible — the very areas, as it happens, with mostly acid hedgebanks of the kind that brambles love — we have ready to hand a substitute range of shrubs, albeit on an awkwardly miniature scale, to which some comparable statistical rule may well apply. In addition, in what I may perhaps term the 'Hooper areas', micro-analysis of the bramble flora could act as a valuable double check.

For this purpose to be able to put a *name* to the species involved is, I suggest, quite superfluous: it is sufficient merely to learn to distinguish them with confidence, maybe jotting down their salient features in a notebook and dubbing them with a letter or number — or even a nickname. A certain proportion, in any case, are almost certain to confound the experts, for there are many local forms still unknown and many that are known but are still without a name. So to wait for the refinement of a scientific nomenclature will be, almost certainly, to wait in vain.

REFERENCES

Allen, D. E., Range patterns in Manx *Rubi, Proc. Bot. Soc. Br. Is.,* 6 (2): 168-169, 1965.

Edees, E. S., Notes on Staffordshire brambles, *Proc. Bot. Soc. Br. Is.,* 1 (3): 301-311, 1955.

Evans, E. Estyn., *Irish Heritage* (pp. 41-42) Dundalk, 1942.

O'Riordain, S. P., Excavations at Cush, Co. Limerick, *Proc. Roy. Irish Acad.,* 45C: 83-181, 1940.

Watson, W. C. R., *Rubi of Great Britain and Ireland,* Cambridge, 1958.